STRIKING
THE DARK AIR
FOR MUSIC

Books by William Pitt Root

STRIKING THE DARK AIR FOR MUSIC

Poems by *William Pitt Root*

New York *1973* *Atheneum*

Some of the poems have been previously published as follows:

ARION'S DOLPHIN (*My Voice is Changing*)
BROWNBAG (*Through This Glass Crowd*)
CAROLINA QUARTERLY (*The Recognition*)
FIRST ISSUE (*The Madder I Get; I'm the Absurd Chameleon*)
FLY BY NIGHT (*Each Day, Each Night; If in a Strong Moment*)
FREE FAMILY NOTES (*Song of Presence*)
GREENSBORO REVIEW (*It's a Terrible Ease*)
INTRO 2 (*I Lie To My Friends; The Moon Set At Midnight; Song of the
    Shedding of Light & Darkness*)
MALAHAT REVIEW (*A Start*)
MENDOCINO DAILY PLANET (*Song of Returnings; Song of Presence*)
THE NATION (*My Lies Become; I Am Owl & Gull*)
NEW VOICES IN AMERICAN POETRY (*The House You Looked For*)
THE NEW YORKER (*Circle of Struggle*)
THE NEW YORKER BOOK OF POEMS (*Circle of Struggle*)
PIPEDREAM PRESS PENNYPAPER (*Song of Emergency; Song of Returnings; Song
    of Presence*)
PLACE (*The House You Looked For*)
POETRY (*Dark Woods; Song of Governance; Song of the Last Hours; Sud-
    denly Your Skull Shocks*)
THE RHODE ISLANDER (*Elegy For Apu*)
SEIZURE (*X/Y*)
STONECLOUD (*Song of When; Song of Choice*)

*For writing grants, my gratitude to Michigan State University, Stanford
University (Stegner Fellowship), the Rockefeller Foundation, and the John
Simon Guggenheim Foundation. For jobs, thanks to University of North
Carolina in Greensboro, Tennessee-Carolina Freightlines, Slippery Rock
State College, Michigan State University, Amherst College, and The Book
Press.*

Thanks to Jean and Carmen at Tai Farm and to everyone at Mayday Farm.

NOTE: *These poems were written and rewritten between winter 1966 and
spring 1972, when I was also finishing most of the work in* ALL'S FAIR,
Poems of Love and War.

This book is for Judy now
and for Jennifer soon.

CONTENTS

Circle of Struggle

Striking The Dark Air For Music

2. Songs From The Rim Of The Wheel Whose Center Is Everywhere

> *"For Beauty's nothing
> but beginning of Terror we're still just able to bear,
> and why we adore it so is because it serenely
> disdains to destroy us."*
>
> R. M. RILKE

CIRCLE
OF STRUGGLE

Deep in the calm of a drawing room of flowers,
the only hand my father held
was dead.
   At twelve
I held my mother's hand
wondering how different mine must feel.
Invisible behind a wreathe of leaves
the Bible shut.
    Her grip tightened
and trembled as her rings cut in our flesh,
and blood came to the edges
of the stones.

This morning, when I had to kill
a mouse to free it
from my trap,
I remembered the rat's gnawed foreleg
my father made me see: sheer bone
protruding from a thin
clenched paw. And this was our secret,
father's and mine, kept
from mother, safe in her kitchen
for years.
                When he died at the verge
of my manhood, she fled north
with me. There I learned the seasons
in a long strange year.
I saw the crippled trees
crumple into colors, shedding
their brilliant disease of leaves
that left the branches dead
and trembling in the snow-white wind,
magical and stark
between streetlamps and starlight.

I learned to set out traps
for muskrats, mink and rabbits—declaring
I would never marry, never.
And each dawn of the long first winter,
silent in the moonlight, I hiked
through the frostbright
dreamlike sleeping trees

that jutted like black bone
from wounded snow. Alone among
the creatured drifts and banks
piled up in the months between
my father's death and my
own beating flesh,
I was fearful and desirous
of the grey silent wolves
a crushed thing's single shriek
could summon from the dark.

With my strong Confederate bayonet
I'd pry slick frozen steel apart,
freeing stiff legs severed
in my traps. Now and then
a worthless skin.

       One morning
early in the wind and while
the blowing moon still wobbled,
jostling the dark fixed trunks
of night, I heard a chain snap tight.
Then beating wings. Something white
was fumbling at the base of the trees.

Like snow rising from snow,
a silver fox locked
in its talons, the great white owl rose,
then fell—dragged back by the trapped weight.
Dazzled by the brightening
air, its lunar eyes blazed
in their mask of blind snow
as I tripped on ice, reared

to meet its stare. It challenged:
I froze.
      White breast wide
with the heavy wings of a warrior
angel, it dipped the hook of its beak
in slow deliberation
and stole a vivid eye from the skull,
then turned to me. Impatient,
in an outburst of brilliance,
it battered up
out of the snow, blindly clumsy at first,
then—transfigured by the high light of ascent—aglide
and glowing
          in the pale soaring sky.

Wet blood, bright
in the decomposing snow,
wound in a desperate
circle of struggle, round
and round the strict radius
of the staked chain.

All around me the horizon tensed
for dawn, encircling my vision
with the limits of a sawtoothed land
sharp against the sky,
and from this trap's dead center
I looked up at the fatal stars
so innocent in their slow prison
of seasons and hours.

This morning, when I
sent my wife and daughter from the room,
they fled as if to witness death
were death itself. *Am I to die?*
—this accusation in their fear
has followed me until
I feel as if my own is the small
nodding skull I've crushed,
and mine the one bright eye
staring from its ruin.
                    So I
am the child again, facing your candor,
knowing this time you must die,
your face pass into my face,
mine into others. What
shall I tell them, father? What can
we tell to these strangers
we have made from our love?

Somewhere,
in the belly of the owl and the earth,
we all stare incessantly from
darkness to darkness soaring.

for Jennifer

I first recognized spring
today: holding
my daughter's flowersmeary hands
in my workwooden hands,

I felt
the green blades cocked
in dry wood
drive free.

ELEGY FOR APU

for Sharon

Apu ben Gasser, Afghan hound
And gentleman, court jester in repose,
But clearly a king once he rose
To stretch or circle in the room, around
And round, until his chosen plot
Of rug was freed of snakes, the grass
Of his imagination tramped flat
As he could make it with his great black feet,

And Apu running, covering the long green ground
As if grace made his body its pure dance
Of speed and beauty, muscles flowing over bone
Concealed beneath deep fur, his elegance
Like water smoothly flexing over stone,

And Apu, who, for his mistress,
Strode across the fields of show and
Stately, at his ease,
Held firm under the judge's hand:

Apu—clown, king, champion,
Gentleman, and friend—

Apu is dead.

In the sideyard, which
he hadn't mowed since moving in,
he sat, reviewing fancies, as sunlight
shaped his body in its shining
skin. He smoked in quiet, tilted
back his head until the sky
was white and sheer, steep with light,
feeling all the wind that pressed him
through the bright hair on his legs
and arms and chest.
                              He nodded, nearly
slept, then a quail exploded
from its nest to the fence's corner post.
The eyes were dark, pearled with sight
and quivering as continental shapes
of black and white turned in orbit
in the socket of the skull. Its head was still.
It clucked and twittered, virtuoso,
while the cock-staff nodded on
its hood, a black note in the wind,
yielding to the fluid motion,
bobbing back to yield again,
back and forth, precise and atremble.
It clucked, waited, chuckled; cocked
its head, clucked again, and flew.
He closed his eyes to listen.
                              Charged
with seed, the tassles of dry grass

creaked among the leaves of weeds
like a wicker chair as someone
sleeps, half sleeps, and stirs. A pair
of grey wrens cleaned dried
bits of berries from their beaks,
tapped and scraped the resonant fence
to whet their bills like dull razors
on strop, then pecked the tall tan loaded
stalks of grass that rose along
the fence's open planks, drooping
and nodding, struck and shattered—broken
for their seed by sudden birds.

He rose to find his pen. The wrens
froze on the fence, flipped and vanished.
The sheen of light that shaped his body
in its own bright armor
disappeared. The wind relaxed;
and when he sat again, he found
his vision's artifacts were gone,
and he was deadlocked between silence
and the moment of shared song.

A NOTE ON NOSTALGIA AS THE CORRUPTION OF INNOCENCE

for Fred

Problematic monsters tyrannize the mapped-out landscape
reeking with itself: the naked ark's aground,
grinding all to hell as the moon pulls
the hull of spirit, pulls
her over shoals of possibility, memory,
gradual corals encrusting her keel
until she's locked there, groaning,
her vital cargo starving in the dead lunar calm.

THE HOUSE YOU LOOKED FOR

I

Upstate New York,
   that haunts me still—beginning
our late fall walk in fields of blown gold weeds
and trees blown red and gold.

That time, that trip to your old home,
I saw you young, heard stories of you young as me,
your knickers stuffed with stolen cookies,
booty to share with kids you fought the day before.
The year you spent in bed, the several months
of dying you did live through.

I was proud and frightened.
You frightened me and made me proud
of what I might become, being your son.

One trip north
and our drive in country so much changed
you couldn't find for hours the place
you'd come for us to find.

II

And now it's merely light wind,
   the long light late in the day,
weeds giving way before you,
   I in your wake in the fields,
seed fastening to my pantlegs, your legs
thrashing free of burrs and the thorns and branches

I was trapped by, you against the sun, you tall
as trees, you graceful with your earned strength moving
    freely.

Then, in a stand of trees the colors of fire,
the house you looked for: sagging roof, broken door
so jammed you had to force it down
with the whole forest looking on
and I looking on.

Inside, cobwebs everywhere. Antique windows
made the light antique as I heard you dressing upstairs
and your mother downstairs calling you
and down the stairs you came.
The stairs collapsing now at the house's center.

III

Father, you could dance
and you learned to dance
with pain. They told you
you couldn't walk again.

Young and sure to die,
you lay and wept, wasting
in the bed of a closed room.
Then changed.
            Changed
with such fierce strength
that curse became command.
You lived despite them all.
You rose, you walked, by god
you danced back into life.

14

I still cry when I hear
how, pale and agonized,
you made them watch you dance.
They did not understand.
You called it dance
and dancing it became.

IV
I will learn that from you.
Your eyes' blue fire burned
with how I came to be.

How true you were, and strong,
and how suddenly gone.

I will redeem your blood.

I promise you your name.

after Rilke

Lord, it is time. Our long summer ends.
Lengthen now Thy shadow on the sundial
and in the farthest fields revolve Thy winds.

Command the last fruits, that they swell and fill.
Give them two days more for their proud weight.
Urge them to fulfillment, then drive the sweet
chosen flesh into the rich wine of the fall.

Now who has no house shall build him none,
who is alone shall long remain alone
to wake and read, to write and read long letters.
Restless, he shall wander up and down
the shrouded avenues where leaves are swirling.

"Estranged. Deeply estranged.

. . . .

hand at the harp without strings
striking the dark air for music,
having no more than the need
to go by."

ROBERT DUNCAN

STRIKING
THE DARK AIR
FOR MUSIC

1. RECKONINGS

*I cannot find the dance
to rid me of this poison.*

I am empty
given to a silence
I despise and need

I make nothing true

When I try to speak
without lies
nothing comes

I cannot bear the silence

My mouth
is a deep lie
crying out

My face a method
of deceit

My hands
lie cruelly
abrupt and graceless

So I hang from my bones
like rotten fruit, bleeding
and sweet
and only half covered by this swarm of words

I lie to my friends
for our comfort

My friends
Year by year they grow richer
these who started out so well

Now clusters of things
like platelets
in their veins
determine their lives

They marry
hate each other
hate hating
and the dying hatred is

They come to me
who am also richer
easier with things
and dying
of hatred and bored
with the dying

And they say to me
Isn't it nice
we still have the same tastes

I lie. I lie by being
one body with one mouth
speaking from two lives, each
supporting one of me,
each destroying one of me.

The blood of two men trying
to be born runs
crazed through my heart. My mind
tries to hold us together, tries
and fails.
    God in the darkness,
how we scream, each
afraid the other will hear how
close to death he's come, fearing
that other who comes through the dark
with shining eyes and the
last contract of mercy clenched
glittering in the dark.

In the silence of the night
we lie together, ghost
clinging ghost for warmth,
haunting this house
with cries that do not come.

My lies become
good pets, admitted
and pampered
by an old lady upstairs
in me. She stirs
from her rocking only
to refill their bowl
with dust urged
from her breast.
Then she'll lace with
crushed glass the bits
of meat made
of the newborn
and tossed at midnight
to the neighbors' beasts
—these she despises
for their size and ominous
good health.
          Nightly
she reviews the subtle
bodies of her own and admires
their perfect grace as her
fingers curl and close
in the painful dark
that keeps her
as she would be kept.

She pulls the shades,
I close my eyes. We sleep,

giving the house entirely
to things that purr
and settle for the warmth
of our still body
and our breath.

Why my obsession with lies

If you could make it
worth my while
I'd take you to the ruins
you with your alien coins

Or maybe you believe I'm one
who fakes credentials, promises
exotic trips
but can't make it
home at night
without losing himself
in every sidestreet and open
mouth on the way

If in a strong moment
I admit to you
I have nothing to say
that is a lie

You know it

But why do you bother
with my miserable offspring
you with your own
scarcely tolerable lives

I cannot bear them
for you

Do what you must

The moon set at midnight
years ago
and still the houses on either side
glow with its dead light

There is nothing to rouse the dogs
and they sleep
in a glitter of dew
cold muzzles buried between paws

Through this glass crowd
stars and the moon
to claim

me the table and page
on page unwritten there

real and dangerous
but nowhere
known yet—a void inarticulate

no way to say it
but it
must be said

heavy cold hard
house of fire

the hand unable
to rouse
unable to please

the pressure
of stars incapable
of meaning

tongue a tin can
brain a box

hand an animal
fierce
hungering and empty

caught between two terminals:

stars beyond time
and the blood feeding now

Up the road three houses
I made a friend.

His eyes are amber set
in raw hamburger.

I spend all day
touching him and talking.

His heavy mouth is inside out,
a meal he never finishes,

lips and tongue interrupted
by blunt teeth.

He smiles as I talk, I'm glad
he cannot help but smile.

I never feed him but at night
he comes smiling

and I hide until morning
when we talk in the new light.

And all night long
sad laughter woke our wives

Friends
you must come again

EACH DAY, EACH NIGHT

I wait
in a house overlooking
a bay full of boats

and the strand
sinking and rising out
of the sea

impatient for something
to come
of haze in the morning

sun in the afternoon
then stars
and the moon

Various lights on the water

I

I'm the absurd chameleon, trying
to match the colors of the fire
    instead of leaping out.

II

The madder I get the calmer I become
until I am a stone
    no one can throw.

Dark woods. A dry
creek running
through dry trees.
Here no hawk can
break through
the loud thrash
of blown leaves
and the dry creek
draws no game
but me. I enter
bringing with me
into this sanctuary
of stunned trees
all the years of
hunger that make
my life a hunt.

My voice is changing
I am changing too

with terrible impatience
that bursts

abruptly on the rocks
rising to shape

my course
with their impediment.

These I would dissolve in my
acceptance of them

if I could—

as a woman taking seed
makes of it

what her body will,
roots

that charge and drain
the altered stone.

The moon like an insect
attracted by the room's light
presses to the window, clings.

Sometimes I am clumsy
with my wife when
she is helpless. But this

is not the moon's
affair: why
should it threaten so?

It grinds against the
glass with its face
like diamonds, trying

to reach me.

I have wakened to the dark
figure of a woman
coming down upon me

eyes wide
in her decomposing face
dead mouth opening

body opening to take
my body in
the seed I cannot hold

against the terrible
thrilling of her need

She turns away I wake
as from a dream
still vivid in the air

First you complain of sleeplessness
and then of dreams

I hear you out
know every cruelty
responsible

Like tin soldiers out trot
the professional
guards of my conscience: I am sorry

for your tears
when you cry out in the dark
turn to feel me there

turn and turn

Suddenly your skull shocks
my cheek with its grating attempt to kiss me
My lips tear flimsy as a child's kite between your teeth
I am a corpse in the third week of my death
startled by our manners
as we disembowel ourselves with the dry bones of our hands
    each claiming something to remember the other by

DECEPTIONS

I

I do not believe you

II

You throw out words like clothes
and my limbs catch them—
coats for men with three arms,
sweaters without armholes.

I will not wear your lies.

I will walk in the grace
of my own perceptions, my body
trained to maneuver unthinkingly
in the lion's skin, my face
the owl's face.

III

My vision is the vision of the hunter,
alert to the fear in others.
I feed on you to maintain my great strength.
How can I love, I who hunger so,
whose blood will not be patient for your blood?

In the dark I move to tear away your soft words,
your warm clothes.
I move in disbelief straight to your heart.

I am Owl & Gull, night & day.
Hungry in the dark & dangerous & joyful.
In the light a fisher, harmless brightwinged ghost crying
    one flat note of sorrow from its prison in the sun.
When the dark comes
my eyes darken for the new world & I set out on short strong
    wings
silent as the moon & stars riding with me in the sky
    & far below I see you
where you call for my soft questions
& the deep quench of my claws.

I take quick comfort
in the glance of dew
the wide stare of the sea

but these things mean
nothing to me
that rouse up everything

A beast roused in its cage
torn on the bars
grinding its teeth on the lock

I cannot tell you

Tonight no moon
but the
memory of your eyes in the dark
hollows of your face

My body drifts, atomic
   cloud of stars lit
for one instant.
   Darkness is on every side
over and under me
   and as this cloud I am
is blown
   I become the dark
background for all beings, myself
   and not myself, having
stayed just long enough
   to see what's coming,
what has been
   and how I pass from
place to place, time
   after time.

Trees of the earth uproot themselves,
crying out dead fruit and the bones of birds.

My bones are a weapon
thrust into me
and into me, spreading
   from the first a formal alien support
     to uphold and shape me,
encasing in my brain
the slow disease of self.

   Can I survive
these bones
I am made upon, left
   in me like the strange spears
     of the stranger enemy? I cannot.
On this painless rack slowly
crazing with sorrows, I must live.

   What a fabulous warfare
life is
as each man struggles
   through the stages of his being
     toward an end so utterly clear
that he interrupts his losses
only to praise them and pass them on.

It's a terrible ease you have with your sorrows,
naming them names and arranging them to make sense of.
The syntax and cadence of grief: what is it?
You're the man handy with words,
a plumber of depths, you say,
but I wouldn't trust you with my pipes. Wrenching
things around like that and screwing up your face
ought to come to something more than these bills for failure.
Receipts. Free admissions.

Crickets.

> *Quizzing*
> *the dark? Singing?*

Scraping their knees.

What good's that,
even for crickets?

About as much good
as your question

or my answer,
or the light in this room.

Compared to the dark.

Without the scraping of knees.

On my wall there's a black and white blown
          up snap of an abandoned
warehouse on Cannery Row.
                    A door torn wide open
on the third floor
opens from nowhere into nowhere
          and above the roof
above the opened door
a pigeon is frozen
          at the instant of ascent out of the dark.

The bird's like me
          sitting here telling
about it:
          it got its start and then was
stopped cold in the camera,
to appreciate the exact
          moment of release, held
forever near the original maw.
Except of course that real birds get away,
          wheeling
     free of all the films we can see.

Enough complaint. Enough
making of dead poems
in the presence of life.

It's spring and all the forms
of life brandish with silly
persistence their leaves, fronds,

buds and legs in an example he
dreads the promises of, threats
he will, he

says, live up to. (He'll take them by their throats
and drink till they inspire
him to follow their sappy examples.) What treats,

what near visions he indulges, tire
s of, runs from. He is fearful.
He brags, is shameful, would like to rear

like a white horse at the cliff's edge but instead will curl
around some soft words, warm
himself against them, hum, knit and purl

the ravelling edges of his
life, ineptly dishonest, incapable of candor,

except in bed, where he fails, sometimes, even at this,

a downfalling lacking
in the fine pierce of splendor.
And he is least a quack when he isn't quacking.

X: You with your fine words and signing my name to your
   poems.

Y: You always find a way out,
worming your fingers through my rib cage,
sticking my tongue out when the jawbone sleeps,
giving my seed into the prison of a woman's hips.
Just what is it you're up to,
an exchange of hostages?

X: You, you are my clothes.

Y: Your poems would be sales slips
for purchases that can't be made.

X: Since when can the sleeve speak for the armpit?
My hands catch in your collarbones.
My legs dangle from the sudden spine impaling my spirit.
When your skeleton started taking root inside me
I knew—I was hardening to death.
You call those changes "formal growth."
But I'm going beyond you.
I want out.

I

Truces. Giving away
my claims to my life
in order
to have my life
permitted one more day.

Rain, rain, when you fall
the sun can shine,
not until.

    Storm, you gather in
    my heart.

II

War, halfhearted you
will fail
to draw blood,
fail to heal. Insist
that each wound
be deeply revealed
to the sun, done with.

III

Cowardice is crueller than any courage.
It wounds and runs away, dragging
apologies to cover all traces.
Back to the lair where it lies
all night, all day,
waiting for a lull
to strike again.

Catch it, beat it down!
Unwind it like a snake's length
from the anchor of its strength, its fantastic alibis.
Skin it out, then leave it to be cured
by its season in the open.

What remains that's worth life will rise up to the dance.

I live now day by hour, by glance and breath
I am content
until the stars rise dragging out the dogs of darkness, my heart
   that bays across their tongues
challenging the stars
as their circles tighten overhead
and my spirit loosens from my bones to take the winds
   of the moon, joyfully deranging in this brilliance
that overwhelms the land of sleepers,
sealed and sane.

Letters. They've
served me
up to now. In them
I could talk
but the talk
was false and
killing me. Now
I write few
and send none.
Nothing I need
to tell can be
made fitting.
The moon and I
have a contract
the sun breaks
into. Grass
withers in its
fields at night.
In the morning
the dew ripens
like berries
in a young
woman's mouth,
running and sweet.

Who could I tell?

SONG BEGGING TO BE BORN

I

No gentle birth, no
easy waking. Years
of my life I've
slept with only this
dream of the world
—that the world
was a dream. That
afraid. Paralyzed
into the poems where
I've nursed the
unacknowledged
passions of my life,
the cutting edge
of death moving surely
even through this dream.

II

You're dying all around me.
You leave me
speaking this calm voice
that records, guts and preserves,
this voice I've dreamed excepts me
when there is no exception.

How can I wake and survive?
To wake now is to die
for the crime of wasting my life
in sleep, reasonable and calm.

III
Wake me!—Wake me now
and to such pain I cannot speak
but must cry out cries so strong
from the roots of their anguish,
roots of their joy,
that my hungers sing!

2. SONGS FROM THE RIM OF THE WHEEL WHOSE CENTER IS EVERYWHERE

I cannot find the house
to hold me when I dance!

SONG OF THE LAST HOURS

The last hours of the year and I am waking
through the slow cold avalanche of night among hills
and houses lost in the dark and glints of
stars uncovered in the rubble of trees and rooves and the
    pointed
ears of dogs alert to the dark
bodies among blind sheets turning
here in movements of sleep or movements of love or turning
at the same time slowly into the earth
among the unconscious dreams of the earthshaping
deep stones, thin seas, wider
insubstantial sky
apparent at all hours—Old skystone,
wheeling around the earth, held in its
circular sway, orbit
innocent of the record it is!

Sometimes fading in the valley at dusk
I watch the high hawks in their circles shine
in the last sunlight, turning
and returning in the deadly orbits
of their craft, overhead
but below the stars and the governance
of their gradual circles.

Loving me, knowing my love
of the colors and smells of fresh flowers,
you used the hours we had here
to sack the garden, plundering
roses and dandelions alike
for the blossoms to please me.

When I returned you to your mother
I came back here and found
the dry vase with its dried bouquet
half on the desktop, half still hanging on.

Now I bring in fresh flowers
and keep the others, too, in their vase of air,
—here fresh flowers and here your promise
for fresh flowers kept constantly
to cheer me.

I

I have been the planner
planned by another

far from me, far,
and me no longer:

The earth around me
turns within my mind

to salt. Its unspeakable
savors arrest me.

Looking backward, forward,
thinking, "There is no difference

between them—the present is
never with me."

Anchor me in this earth
that I may live,

whoever loves me!

II
Moving, I love moving
through space

but time appalls me.
I grow dim, fade.

Praise God life's not
a highwire act: I am a bear

as clumsy off the ground
as I am strong among trees.

III
Look backward, look forward,
what is there to see?

I lived once with my own fears
and my wife's

and I moved on. Moved on
but stopped

for one look back,
and froze.

Break me, for godsake
break me down!

Anger me with love now,

not with caution. Charity

is such a murder. Don't hang
back from me.

IV
I have lived waiting for the blade
to fall.

I could not hide.
The blade was in myself.

Blade was myself.
Self fell: what bonds were cut?

What, whole and shining with strength,
will stride now from its prison

out into eternity?

v

Here there are roses,
planted and tended

by the hands of men.
Berries in the hedges

cluster bright and red.
This is a new year.

I am a new man.
These are new tears.

SONG OF THE VINES RIPENING

For months the bare vines
winding through the trellis
have been hung with long dark pods
whose down caught
light from the sun and moon.

Today as I wrote you, puzzling
what to say, and how,
something clicked at my window.
I looked, no one was there.

Then
the window again. But this time
two brown beans shot through.
The pods—they were bursting, showering beans
to the earth
and the floor of my room. Dried and shrunken
beyond bearing, they burst and flung
    out seeds like shouts of joy,
like these astonished words
I give you now.

SONG OF A BLIND TRAVELLER

As a blind man negotiates
rutted backroads, marvelling,
if he maintains his balance,
at his grace, so some men
leaning upon fences on the way
will amuse themselves
with the clumsiness they see,
while others, witnessing
his grace,
will share grace with him.

SONG OF COORDINATES

I look out across clouds,
breathe the hard simple air.

Whistle of a rockchuck.

Shadow of a hawk.

Hole in the earth.

SONGS OF VANITY: A LANDSCAPE OF VOICES

WATER

I am the water always,
clear and easy
for the creatures in me.
Never the same twice,
particle by particle I sink,
I rise. Always
the body of me stays.

I am the shining on the grass,
the twinkling of stars,
the ghosts from drowning fires,
tears, the brilliancy of eyes.
I answer thirst
or thirst has no answer.

Sky breathes me,
earth drinks me,
stones deny me
and I wear down stones.
Roots search for me,
I give myself to roots
and in that transport rise,
blossom and expire.

I feed you—I feed all life
streaming to the sea—
yet feed just upon myself.

I am with you at your birth,
attend you throughout life,
abandon you at death.

And I am water always.

LIGHT

You cannot see me
and I show you
everything you know.

I have no weight, no substance
yet
my effects are apparent everywhere.

I am constant,
various.

Too much of me
and you are blind
and too little
blind.

I am always on my way
beyond you, moving
as your bones beat once
farther than your numbers dream.

I am light.

AIR

I am the air.
Everywhere we
marry.

Every breath.

I am the child of light and water
passing through me
to themselves again.

I am vast and negligible,
scarcely there,
essential.

What I do not touch now
I have touched,
what I touch now
will be taken from me
and be back,
unearthed.

I am waiting.

Even to the grave I go
with the body,
whose gradual exhalation
frees me.

Take a deep breath,
hold it,
we
are becoming one.

POND

I am the pond, nothing
but other things
—water, air, the light.
I occur
when they meet here.

How can I speak
when I cannot imagine
I am real?—
I am a convention,
a crude one.

Define me with a measurement,
a volume,
brilliance, weight
—whatever means you wish—,
by the time you describe me
I am otherwise.

Springs increase me, freshen me.
The sun heats and robs me.
Creatures in me move,
the clouds on my surface shift,
I sink into the earth,
rise through the air.
Here one season,
in another, gone.

But if we do not worry so
with words,
you may enter into me with your whole being.

HERON

I am the heron.

I see you below me,
see you at a distance
in the tall grass,
watching.

You cannot approach me.
I am sensible and shy.
You're careless
with what you cannot use
—you cannot use me.

Among my own
life is a dire blessing,
simple, unreflective.
We join to court and breed,
play and fight, rear
our young and part.
We speak only to warn or summon,
to comfort.

We are silent.
We fish.

Yet I would starve
before I'd strike at the small fish
swimming there
in the reflection of your face.

After dreaming the pure pleasure
of a being loose in clear water,
diving easily in and out
of the warm mud deep at the bottom,
I wake to the risks of light.

I kick free and I streak
joyous as a bird toward the sun
out of the earth, through water, into the air
where I hang for an instant
free of awareness of safety, free of danger
in the dominion of the heron.

From this height
I glimpse at a distance, tall and white,
the still gods where they bend
above the pond or hunch in trees
to dry those wings spread glowing in the sun.
They stare into the shallows.
They shine like clouds.

At night I have slept dreaming
    of those reed-legged gods whose eyes are small suns,
who are silent
    but whose rare calls pierce my world like claws,
who fly as we dream of flying
    and burn against the sun in a great tumult of wings,

whose slow grace threatens us
    and wooes us with its beauty,
who consume us to survive,
    whose lives we dread and envy.

Now I wait the moment when,
suspended above the midworld of water,
I will know the presence of the white cloud lowering,
the explosive sun quick
above the pierce of the beak,
the shrieking wings.

The first gift was hilarity as language vanished and my senses were restored.

The second gift was the free place I knew wholly down to the vibrance of the scales of each fish swimming the brook through the valley of grasses.

The third gift was the hand darkness offered from darkness, with knowledge that to hold the hand was comfort and silenced the moaning and that my efforts to pull it into the light were violations of love with no success possible.

The fourth gift was the vision of my loved ones dead with age and beyond me forever and the chance to ask my own corpse a single question.

The fifth gift was fire: In that fire I burned without even the promise of death to relieve my anguish.

The sixth gift was release from pain and access to eternal energy.

The seventh gift was grace.

The last gift was re-entry into language and the loss of all previous gifts into memory, for the final gift restored my citizenship in Babel.

SONG OF CHOICE

silence
blessing
calling me when I am lost
W. S. MERWIN

I

That man, standing there in the field,
his head hived with light
the colors of flowers,
his brain honeycombed with scent,
his tongue silent, tasting silence
—His presence is a marriage
with the earth and sky now,
each breathing moment
a treasury of delight.

II

He cannot talk. Speech
betrays
everything precious he knows.
He tries, but he cannot talk.
Lies, all lies, speech
breeding sorrow if believed,
mistrust if not. What he has
is his because it is all
around him everywhere always.

III

Speech divorces him from the earth.
Silence cuts him off from men.
These, for a time, are his choices.

Today out in the woods
an old tree found me.
It said *I am you*

and a chorus of whispers
blew by where I shook.

I am you it said
with no words, no words.

Big tree, dead, huge memory
of itself collapsing
to feed the green shoots
ringing its base,

and the babble of whispers
blew by where I listened,

their small voices hard
to hear:

> *we* they seemed to say
> *we*
> *are becoming you.*

And the shaking stopped.—

O when I stood up walking
through the wall of light
and moved across the hill
down into the waterfall
what could my face say
to the visible glory of your face
and your eyes shining?

Grasses, Stones and Trees,
Sunshine and Cider,

—Hello, River!

I have moved
forever.

I am all appetite
a net flung to catch fish
that catches stars

SONG OF RECOGNITION

After the long letters
have been written, read,
abandoned, after
distances grow absolute
and speech, too,
is distance, only
listening is left.

I have heard the dark hearts
of the stones
that beat once in a lifetime.

I let go of my darkness I have grieved there & been lost

I lay down in greenshining grasses smelling of them & rolling
    in them
I wake up in the dew where innumerable worlds orient &
    balance
    the sun recurring in each drop rounded by the light
    Earth rounded by our star's radiance
I wake up to the water wake up light wake dew grass &
    stones
    wake eyes & ears wake the pink cloud of my bones
    & old loves & new fulfill my spirit's waking

I wake up, Lord
I wake up to this blazing coat of joys
    no grief destroys

SONG OF RETURNINGS

All the bones of the horses rise in moonlight
on the flatlands, dropping
from trees, squeezing out from
under rocks, disengaging themselves
from the earth and things that live from the earth
and the scattered uniforms assemble
   to the sounds of bugling come back from the stars
and what has rotted into dust reforms with a furious sound
   of whirlwind tearing the faces from the astonished living
and gold flows molten from the mouth of Cortez
   and returns to the stones and the water and the air
and the redwoods collapse back into cones
and Christ is pried from the cross and flogged and spat upon
   and let loose among fishermen who scatter to their ships
   and enters his mother's womb and enters into the stars
and Babylon reassembles and Sodom and Gomorrah reassemble
and David sings then babbles in his mother's arms
and all living things return to their sources
and the waters return to their sources
and the sun returns to the source
and the vast darkness returns
and all things are
and are not.

SONG OF SHEDDING LIGHT
AND DARKNESS

Stars
 stars
 and grass deepening
the dark fields

No one
 walks here
 with me and I feel
the hillside moving

as I move
 enclosed
 by stars, abrasive
and careless, turning

around me
 grinding
 light and the darkness
from my skin, skin

from my
 bones until
 blind and clean
I am ready to go on

SONG OF WHAT THE RAIN SAID

Rain speaks to the grass.

I overhear it
and my ears get wet.

May light sweeten in your lungs
may your tongue shine

May you be grateful to your body
for the offenses it forgives you
may your body please you
may your mind accept its forms
and guide you among dangers and pleasures

May you love yourself as you are loved